Survival Kit

Learn how to choose key verses, memorize word-perfect, ensure long term retention recall references, meditate effectively, and more...

Five Challenging Bible Searches
Ten Bible-Based Keys to Memorizing
Weekly Objectives for Small Groups
Everything You Need To Begin!

WWW.FASTMISSIONS.COM

Copyright © 2022 by Dan Vis
All rights reserved
including the right of reproduction
in whole or in part in any form.

All Scripture quotations are from the
King James Version of the Bible
Emphasis supplied unless otherwise indicated.

ISBN: 978-0-9821805-5-6

Published by FAST Missions
111 2nd Street
Kathryn, ND 58049

Additional copies of this book are available by
visiting us at WWW.FAST.ST

Survival Kit
Course Content

The FAST *Survival Kit* is the first step in our three part training process designed to help you take in, live out, and then pass on the Word of God. It gives you all the keys you need to begin memorizing Scripture effectively. You will learn how to memorize word-perfect, ensure longterm retention, meditate, apply, remember references and more.

This course consists of five weeks of instruction. It includes weekly objectives, five Bible searches, assigned memory verses, and two memory keys for each study. The titles in this series include:

1. Amazing Grace
2. Looking to Jesus
3. Tackling Temptation
4. The Road Ahead
5. Fellowship of Faith

Please visit us online for supplemental resources including week by week teaching tips, promotional materials, quizzes, exams, certificates, memorization tools, and much more. You can also take this course in our online school: learn with students from around the world, ask questions, and interact with the author. For more information, please go to *WWW.FAST.ST/SK-GIFT*.

Amazing Grace

Week #1

Amazing Grace
Survival Kit > Week 1 > Memo

F

A

S

T

Memo:

Hi! Welcome to the FAST Survival Kit—a simple little program designed to give you a taste of what it really means to be a joy-filled Christian. This lesson you are about to start is the first of five. Once you have completed them all, you will not only know what it takes to survive as a Christian—you will know how to thrive!

Put a little effort into these studies. You will learn a lot, and they will help deepen your walk with God. You will also gain something invaluable: keys to memorizing Scripture effectively.

You see, there is power in the Word of God. It has spoken entire worlds into existence. It has overthrown kingdoms and it has raised the dead. In fact, God's Word is so powerful, it never returns void—it always accomplishes what it sets out to do. (See Isaiah 55:11).

Start laying up that kind of power in your heart, and your whole life will begin to change. Try it, and see! Turn the page to begin...

**The Editor,
Hid in Christ**

Amazing Grace
Survival Kit > Week 1 > Objectives

Name: _____   Initialed by: _____

Date: _____

- ❑ Our first Bible Search is titled **Amazing Grace**. Simply read the questions, look up the verses in a Bible, and then answer the questions in your own words. Pause a moment before beginning and ask God to speak through His Word as you study. Think of this first Bible Search as a brief introduction to God. May it give you fresh insights into what He is really like.

- ❑ Your first memory verse is **Jeremiah 31:3**. Write out this week's verse on a card and slide it into a verse pack as described in Key #1. Then, follow the suggestions in Key #2 to begin memorizing it. Get to the point where you can quote this verse *word-perfect*. Both cards and packs are available in our Online Store. Or if you prefer, use our FREE digital tools at *WWW.FAST.ST*.

- ❑ Look for the section of this lesson entitled **Practical Suggestions**. There you will discover our first two secrets to memorizing effectively. Read this information carefully. By the end of this program, your goal will be to know all ten—in order. So begin learning these first two keys right away. Memorizing God's Word is an exciting adventure—are you ready?

I rejoice at thy word,
As one that findeth great spoil.
Psalms 119:162

Amazing Grace
Survival Kit > Week 1 > Bible Search

Welcome to the first Bible Search in our FAST Survival Kit. The five studies in this program will look at those basics of the Christian life that are essential to your long term success and happiness. Bible Search One looks at what God is really like, and what it means to be a son or daughter of God. Press on with a prayer in your heart, and enjoy.

> *The LORD hath appeared of old unto me, saying, Yea, I have loved thee with an everlasting love: therefore with lovingkindness have I drawn thee. Jeremiah 31:3*

1. How does the Bible introduce God? Genesis 1:1

2. How is God involved in our world today?

    Nehemiah 9:6

    Lamentations 3:22-23

Note: God is not some giant clockmaker that simply wound up the universe and then left it alone to run down by itself. Rather, the Bible describes our Creator as intimately involved in our continued existence, preserving and sustaining us, day by day.

3. What do each of the following verses tell us about God?

   Psalms 90:2

   I Chronicles 29:11-12

   Romans 11:33

   Note: The God of the Bible is described as eternal, all powerful, and infinitely wise. As Jesus once said, "With God all things are possible" (Matthew 19:26).

4. What is the special object of God's attention?

   Psalms 139:1-6

   Luke 12:6-7

   Note: God's attentive interest is on you and your life—much like a loving parent, watching, waiting to encourage and help. Jesus once said, "Fear not, little flock; for it is your Father's good pleasure to give you the kingdom" (Luke 12:32).

5. What are God's thoughts toward us? Jeremiah 29:11

Note: God has a special plan for our individual happiness and is waiting only for our cooperation to bring it to pass!

6. What do the following verses suggest about God's plan for our lives?

   Psalms 84:11

   Psalms 37:4

   Romans 8:32

   Note: God wants nothing but the best for us, and will withhold no blessing from those who live for Him.

7. How should we respond to God's plans for our lives? Hebrews 11:6

   Note: The human response to God's initiatives which pleases Him most is faith! We should look forward with anticipation to the unfolding of God's will for our life!

8. What does Jesus say about faith in the following verses?

   Matthew 9:29

   Mark 9:23

   Note: There is, it seems, an underlying law of the universe: that the fulfillment of God's plan for our life is directly connected to our faith in God's longing to make us successful and happy.

9. In light of the facts we have studied so far, what emotion should fill our heart? Philippians 4:4

Isn't it incredible? God not only created you, but He has the deepest love for you, and an abiding interest in every detail of your life. What is more, God has a rich plan for your life, designed specifically for your happiness—and He's willing to use all the resources of heaven to ensure that plan comes to pass! Do you believe it? Enough to respond with thanksgiving and joy? Even when things seem the bleakest? Why not choose today, to pursue God's best for your life—by faith!

❏ Yes   ❏ No

Amazing Grace
Survival Kit > Week 1 > Practical Suggestions

In the weeks to come, the FAST Survival Kit will introduce you to ten keys to successful Scripture memory—drawn directly from the Bible. We strongly recommend that you follow these principles closely, especially when starting out. Scripture memory does not have to take much time or effort, and it can quickly become the joy and rejoicing of your heart—but there are some helpful principles you should understand. Our first two keys are listed below:

Key #1. Use Good Tools.

> *If the iron be blunt, and he do not whet [sharpen] the edge, then must he put to more strength: but wisdom is profitable to direct.*
> *Ecclesiastes 10:10*

Just as a sharp axe enables you to chop the same amount of wood with less energy, a good Scripture memory tool can give you a better return on your investment of time and effort. Perhaps the best tool around is a small verse pack—with verse cards—that fits easily in your pocket. Both cards and packs can be obtained at many Christian bookstores—or from FAST.

Simply write the verse you want to memorize and its reference on one side of a verse card, and then just the reference on the back. Next, slide the card into the clear outside pocket of your verse pack with the words of the verse facing out. If you keep your verse pack with you, you can pull it out any time you have a few minutes and work on a verse: walking down a sidewalk, sitting at a stoplight, waiting in line, etc. Redeem such moments carefully, and you will be able to learn countless verses without having to set aside special times for memorizing. Slipping your verse pack into a pocket each morning will soon be as much a habit as grabbing your wallet or keys.

If you are gadget kind of person—and usually have your phone handy, FAST offers a free digital verse pack you can use, that does essentially the same thing. You simply enter any verses you want to learn, and then access them with a single tap on your phone–anytime, anywhere. It also has the several built in memorization tools to help you learn your verses. You can check this tool out at *WWW.FAST.ST/VP*.

Key #2. Memorize Word-Perfect.

> *Ye shall not add unto the word which I command you, neither shall ye diminish ought from it, that ye may keep the commandments of the LORD your God which I command you. Deuteronomy 4:2*

God's Word is sacred, and we should be very careful to memorize each "jot and tittle" of it accurately. Take care lest you inadvertently add to, or take away from God's Holy Word. It is also important in terms of memorization itself. The more perfectly you memorize a verse—the more firmly it is engraved in your brain. A later lesson will look at the importance of reviewing recently memorized verses. You will discover it is essential to review a verse exactly the same way every time in order to get it into your permanent memory banks—so learn it right, the first time. Remember, it takes no more effort to memorize a verse correctly than it does to memorize it wrong! In short, make it a rule to always memorize your verses word-perfect.

To memorize a verse, simply repeat the first phrase of the verse several times until you can say it from memory. Then add the next phrase, quoting them together until both are fixed in your mind. Continue working at it, one phrase at a time, until you can quote the entire verse: word-perfect. It may be necessary to relearn the verse several times over the next few days, but each time it will get easier, and eventually it will begin to stick. Work at it a little every day, and God will bless your efforts.

You are off to a good beginning! Start using a verse pack and learn your first verse. Remember—use little spare moments throughout the day, and memorize each verse accurately. We'll share more keys to successful Bible memorization in our next study.

Looking to Jesus

Week #2

Looking to Jesus
Survival Kit > Week 2 > Memo

F
A
S
T

Memo:

Hi! Welcome back once again to the FAST Survival Kit. We pray this program will give you valuable insights into joyous Christian living. Insights that make a real difference. Insights that work.

This week you will study the secret to power in the Christian life. The apostle Paul once said "though our outward man perish, yet the inward man is renewed day by day" (II Corinthians 4:16). There was an inner strength that enabled Paul to press through the most trying circumstances victoriously. And that strength is available to us! It comes through fellowship with Christ.

You will also learn some additional principles of Scripture memory. Peter says the Word of God is incorruptible seed, and that it lives and abides forever. (I Peter 1:23). It is not your typical book!

But like all seed, it must be planted. It must sink down deep into our heart, if it is to germinate. Think about it. Scripture memory is planting living, incorruptible seed.

**The Editor,
Hid in Christ**

Looking to Jesus
Survival Kit > Week 2 > Objectives

Name: _____   Initialed by: _____

Date: _____

- ❏ How did you do on your first Bible Search? This week our Bible Search is titled **Looking to Jesus**. It explores what it really means to follow Christ. Before you begin, make sure you ask God to show you great things in the Word. Claim Jeremiah 33:3. How wonderful it is that the true Author of the book is available to explain it!

- ❏ Your memory verse this week is **John 15:5**. Write out a card, put it in the outside pocket of your verse pack, and slide last week's verse into an inside pocket. As you work on your new verse, make sure you don't forget the old one. Review them both at least once each day—until you can quote both word-perfect.

- ❏ Your **Practical Suggestions** this week give two of our most exciting memory keys. They talk about how to draw the meaning out of a verse and then connect it to one's daily life. Once a person learns to meditate on Scripture and apply it practically, the Bible becomes a whole new book! Review these keys daily, along with the first two—until you can recite all four in order, by heart.

The entrance of thy words giveth light;
It giveth understanding unto the simple.
Psalms 119:130

Looking to Jesus
Survival Kit > Week 2 > Bible Search

How did you do on Bible Search One? It is vital to our Christian survival that we have a genuine faith in God's longing to do great things for us in our life! This lesson focuses on an equally important key to Christian survival—the renewing power of a mind centered on Christ. Begin the lesson with prayer, and enjoy your study.

I am the vine, ye are the branches: He that abideth in me, and I in him, the same bringeth forth much fruit: for without me ye can do nothing. John 15:5

1. What did Jesus say needs to happen to every person? John 3:3

Note: The new birth experience is absolutely indispensable to Christian living. As Jesus went on to explain: "that which is born of the flesh is flesh; and that which is born of the Spirit is spirit!"

2. When asked, "How can these things be?" Jesus used a story from the Old Testament to explain the new birth. What was that story? John 3:14-15

Note: Jesus used an ancient story from the days of Moses to illustrate the deep spiritual truth of how a man is born again!

3. What was the key to "survival" in the story Jesus referred to? Numbers 21:8-9

Note: Though "faith" and "belief" are sometimes vague concepts, the word "look" is easy to understand. We instinctively grasp what it means to turn our eyes and look.

4. How do each of the following verses express this same principle?

   Isaiah 45:22

   Hebrews 12:1-2

   II Corinthians 3:18

   Note: Over and over we are instructed to just look. Come and see!

5. What is one way we can fix our spiritual attention on Jesus? John 5:39

   Note: Though we cannot physically see Jesus, we can study the Bible and fix our focus on His life through the Word. The Scriptures are like a mirror reflecting Christ to all who look. See II Corinthians 3:18.

6. What is the result of an encounter with Christ through the Scriptures? Luke 24:32

Note: While there are many reasons to study—the most important is that experience of fellowship with Christ, enriching and warming the heart.

7. How often should we have this kind of encounter? II Corinthians 4:16

Note: Our spiritual survival is dependent upon our daily pursuit of fellowship with Christ through prayer and the study of His Word!

8. According to the following verses, why is this daily renewing of the mind so important?

   Romans 12:2

   II Corinthians 4:16-18

   Ephesians 4:23-24

Note: Our faithfulness in looking to Christ and experiencing a daily renewal of our mind is key to the transformation of our lives. We must never lose sight of this important truth!

9. What priority should we place on beholding Christ?

   Psalms 27:4

   Philippians 3:8

   Note: As Paul once wrote, "for me to live is Christ" (Philippians 1:21). We should all strive to reach this point.

10. What lesson will we learn in putting Christ first? Philippians 4:13

It has been said that the word "Christian" simply means someone with "Christ in" them, and it's true. But for many, there is little real power. The secret to experiencing authentic Christian living is learning to keep our eyes fixed on Jesus. Day by day, study the Word, meet with Christ, and allow your heart to be warmed. If you do, you will soon find yourself growing more and more like the Savior. You will grasp more clearly, both your great dependence on Him and your great power in Him. Christ will become the center of your life—and it will be evident to everyone around you. And isn't that the longing of your heart?

❏ Yes   ❏ No

Looking to Jesus
Survival Kit > Week 2 > Practical Suggestions

This week we will be looking at two of the most important keys to successful Scripture memorization. You see, it is not enough to just know how to memorize a verse—you must also learn how to get into the meaning of the verse, and then build that verse into your life. These skills are called meditation and application. We pray you find the suggestions below helpful.

Key #3. Learn to Meditate.

Meditate upon these things; give thyself wholly to them; that thy profiting may appear to all. I Timothy 4:15

Some of the greatest blessings in the Bible are promised to those who learn to meditate on Scripture day and night. Who are constantly thinking about what some verse says. To do this certainly requires memorization—you don't always have your Bible open in front of you—but it takes much more. You must learn how to chew on a verse, prayerfully, and draw out the principles contained within it. Here are some suggestions:

- Ask yourself questions: Who is speaking in the verse, and to whom? What is he trying to communicate—and why? What makes this verse important? What insights does this verse give you? How does it make you feel?

- Try emphasizing individual words in a verse. What meaning does each key word contribute to the verse? Are there other words that mean the same thing—but give you clearer insight into what the verse is really saying?

- Draw connections between this verse and other verses you know, or have read before. What light do they shed on each other? The more verses you know, the more exciting these connections will become!

- Say the verse back to God in prayer, and talk to Him about what it really means. And specifically: what it says about you, and what it says about Him. Use the verse to deepen your relationship with God.

Key #4. Apply the Word.

But be ye doers of the word, and not hearers only, deceiving your own selves. James 1:22

Meditation should always be combined with personal application. Application is simply taking the principles you see in a verse, and then finding ways to implement them. It seeks to integrate a verse into one's daily life. It looks for practical steps to put a verse into action. Its goal is to experience the verse. Here are some tips to get you started:

- *Goals.* Does this verse have any bearing on your goals? Your direction in life? The things you are working toward? Perhaps it will suggest a way to move forward toward a goal, or it may suggest altering, or even eliminating a goal.

- *Decisions.* All of us face challenging decisions at times. Does this verse shed light on any decisions you are facing? Does it point to some choice you should make?

- *Lifestyle.* Think through your daily schedule. Your habits, patterns, and routines. Can you think of ways to change your lifestyle—that would bring it more into harmony with the verse you are memorizing?

- *Problems.* Are there any difficulties or irritations in your life? Perhaps the verse will suggest solutions. Look for answers to the perplexing problems of your life.

Ask God to impress you with at least one project for every verse you memorize—something small you can do to help build that verse into your life. Try to make sure that these projects are clearly connected to the verse you are memorizing, that they are specific, and that they are small enough to be carried out that day or soon thereafter.

Tackling Temptations

Week #3

Tackling Temptation
Survival Kit > Week 3 > Memo

F

A

S

T

Memo:

How are you doing so far? Have you been giving this program your best? Are you memorizing your verses? Completing your Bible Searches? Learning your memory keys? More important, are you putting what you learn into practice? These lessons cover vitally important topics. Get everything out of them you can.

Jesus once used an interesting parable to explain the importance of hiding God's Word in the heart. "The kingdom of heaven," He said, "is like unto leaven, which a woman took, and hid in three measures of meal, till the whole was leavened" (Matthew 13:33).

You see, once you start hiding the Word in your heart it begins to work—little by little—until the whole life is transformed. It doesn't all happen at once, but it does start at once! So get into the Word. Press forward in your memorization of the Bible. Get all the spiritual leaven you can!

**The Editor,
Hid in Christ**

Tackling Temptation
Survival Kit > Week 3 > Objectives

Name: _____   Initialed by: _____

Date: _____

- ❑ Hope you are enjoying your Bible Searches. This week's study is called **Tackling Temptation**, and looks at the problem of sin. Temptations come to each of us—how important then, that we learn to deal with them correctly! "Tackle" this study with prayer.

- ❑ This week's memory verse is a favorite to many: **I John 1:9**. Take some time to think it through. What two blessings does it promise? What are the conditions? What does it say about the character of God? Use your meditation skills to gain all the insights into this verse you can. Review your other verses daily until you can quote all three word-perfect.

- ❑ Your next memory keys discuss how to move a verse from your short term memory to your long term memory. Imagine—not only being able to memorize a verse, but being able to retain it! You will also discover how to remember references. It's not hard: just read this week's **Practical Suggestions** and follow them closely. Continue reviewing all six keys daily. (You may wish to write them out on a verse card and keep the list in your verse pack). Four more keys to go!

Through thy precepts I get understanding:
Therefore I hate every false way.
Psalms 119:104

Tackling Temptation
Survival Kit > Week 3 > Bible Search

Though God has a great plan for our life (Bible Search One), and all the riches of heaven are available to us through Christ (Bible Search Two), sometimes we stumble. Temptation sneaks in, sin overwhelms us, guilt weighs us down. Fortunately, God has made provision for just such occasions, and understanding that provision is vital—to our survival.

If we confess our sins, he is faithful and just to forgive us our sins, and to cleanse us from all unrighteousness. I John 1:9

1. What is one problem the Bible describes as common to all? I Corinthians 10:13

Note: Our greatest temptation is to allow the things of this world to divert our focus from Christ.

2. What is the source of this problem? James 1:13-15

Note: From the point of birth, we are locked in mortal combat with the sin nature inside us, pressuring us to yield to the appeal of temptation. That struggle does not vanish on becoming a Christian.

3. Is victory possible, and from where? I Corinthians 15:57

Note: Praise the Lord! Though temptation may rage, victory can be won—through Christ! Strive to keep your focus on Him.

4. What is the first step to take when we stumble into and fail some temptation?

   Proverbs 28:13

   I John 1:9

   Note: All too often our natural response is to deny, excuse, justify, or otherwise minimize our behavior. But freedom comes only in facing the truth about ourselves head on. As Jesus once said, "Ye shall know the truth, and the truth shall make you free." (John 8:32)

5. How did Paul describe genuine repentance? II Corinthians 7:10-11

   Note: Repentance is more than just acknowledging sin; it is a deep sorrow for sin, and a resolute desire to turn away from it. This kind of repentance comes only from God—so if you find yourself struggling with some cherished sin, ask for the gift of true repentance.

6. How does God respond to true confession and repentance? Psalms 103:10-14

Note: God is clearly willing to forgive—and treat us as if we had never sinned. The tougher question, often, is whether we are willing to forgive ourself and accept God's free offer to begin afresh.

7. What else should we pray for after stumbling into sin?

   Psalms 51:10

   Ezekiel 36:27

   II Corinthians 5:17

   Note: God's Word is full of wonderful promises for victory over sin. Lay hold of these verses and claim them for yourself!

8. According to Peter, what are the promises in God's Word able to do? II Peter 1:4. See also Psalms 119:11

   Note: The promises of Scripture are the key to escaping temptation! When hid in the heart, and mixed with faith—sin's power is broken.

9. How many times do you think God is willing to forgive you? Matthew 18:21-22

Note: While God is holy and expects obedience, He is also patient and remembers our frame, that we are dust. Even if you have stumbled repeatedly—put your hope in God. Seek Him with all your heart, and victory will come. Jeremiah 29:12-13.

10. What will God ultimately empower you to do? Jude 1:24

Friend, is there some sin in your life causing guilt? frustration? despair? Don't give up! Victory is possible through Christ, and in God's perfect timing and in His own gentle way, He will reveal to you what you need to know to overcome. For now, be honest, confess your sin to God, and repent. Then lay hold on God's Word—both His promise to forgive and His promise to cleanse. Both are crucial if you want to survive! Are you willing to press forward with undimmed courage in your personal battle with temptation?

❏ Yes   ❏ No

Tackling Temptation
Survival Kit > Week 3 > Practical Suggestions

Ready for more keys to Bible memorization? This week we will look at two more important principles: how to get a verse from your short term memory banks into your permanent ones, and then how to remember references—where the verse is found. Follow these suggestions carefully, and they will revolutionize your memorization.

Key #5. Focus on Retention.

> *He taught me also, and said unto me, Let thine heart retain my words: keep my commandments, and live. Get wisdom, get understanding: forget it not; neither decline from the words of my mouth. Proverbs 4:4-5*

God wants us to not only memorize His Word, but to "engrave" it in our mind. He wants us to retain it, keep it, hold it fast, and never forget it. We are to give "earnest heed" to our verses, "lest at any time we should let them slip" (Hebrews 2:1). After all, why invest time memorizing a verse you will just go on to forget a day or two later? The secret, of course, is an effective review system. Here is what we suggest:

Once you have memorized a verse, date it, and put it together with other recently memorized verses in one of the inside pockets of your verse pack. (The other pocket is for blank cards). Review this group of verses every day—preferably during your morning study time. Don't miss a day! Look at the side of the card with only the reference, quote the verse, and then turn the card over to check your accuracy. After a couple of weeks a verse will become easy to quote—but don't stop there! It will take a full two months to get the verse permanently engraved in your brain.

Once the date indicates a verse has been in your daily review for two months, move it to a permanent back review file that you keep at home. Work through these verses at least once a week, at first. Later, after you have accumulated several hundred verses, you may wish to move your better-known verses to a section for monthly review. Do this consistently, and every verse will stay sharp, right on the tip of your tongue. And if a verse does get a bit rusty, just give it some extra attention: slip it in with your daily or weekly review verses for a while. It will soon spring back to life—fresh as ever!

To help with your memorization, FAST has a powerful review engine that automates the entire review process. We strongly recommend it. For more information, check it out at *WWW.FAST.ST/ENGINE*.

Just think: if you memorize two verses a week, and use an effective review system, you will have over one hundred verses in less than a year. In ten years you will have over a thousand! Imagine—a thousand verses all perfectly engraved in your mind, and right on the tip of your tongue! It can happen.

Key #6. Know your References.

> *Study to shew thyself approved unto God, a workman that needeth not to be ashamed, rightly dividing the word of truth.*
> *II Timothy 2:15*

You should not only know what a verse says—but also where it is found. It's not enough to be able to quote it, you must be able to turn to it in your Bible and show it to a friend. Many people struggle with remembering references, but it's not that hard, if you just follow these simple suggestions:

First, make sure you learn the reference with the verse. One way to do that is what I call "reference glue" Basically, try saying the reference, and just the first part of the verse rapidly, ten or more times–until it sticks. And then repeat as often as needed. Basically, it sounds like this:

> I John 1:9, If we confess our sins...
> I John 1:9, If we confess our sins...
> I John 1:9, If we confess our sins...

Second, when doing your daily review, always quote the reference before and after the verse--every time. Think of it like a sandwich: reference, verse, reference. This cements the verse to the reference and vice versa. So when you hear the reference, you think of the verse. And when you hear the verse, you think of the reference. It works!

And third, even more fun, our review engine has special reference drills you can do to keep all those verse locations sharp. Give it a try!

Knowing the references of your verses is an important part of your memorization. Follow these tips and you'll be sure to succeed.

The Road Ahead

Week #4

The Road Ahead
Survival Kit > Week 4 > Memo

F
A
S
T

Memo:

Hi! Welcome back once again. We pray this program is proving a blessing to you—giving you rich insights into the Christian life. This study looks at another vital area: how to discern God's direction for your life. If you have ever wondered how to know God's will, answers are just ahead!

And while we do not know God's exact plans for your life, we do know this: there is no limit to what God can do with one person who will give himself fully to Christ and make room for the working of His Spirit in his heart. No limit!

We know this too: that God's plan for your life is spelled out in His Word. All the instructions you need are there, waiting for you to just dig in and find them. You will find promises to claim, counsel to follow, and warnings to heed. And it's full of great ideas!

Yes, it's all there—in the Word. So do what it takes to get as much of that Word into your heart as you can!

**The Editor,
Hid in Christ**

The Road Ahead
Survival Kit > Week 4 > Objectives

Name: _____   Initialed by: _____

Date: _____

❏ Your Bible Search this week is another important one. It is called **The Road Ahead**, and looks at how to discern God's leading in your life. God has great plans for each of us, but we must learn to tune into His leading in order for His plans to be fulfilled perfectly. We pray this study helps.

❏ Are you ready for your next verse? Have you learned your first three thoroughly? Remember, you should be reviewing each of these verses at least once a day. It should only take a minute or two to review them, but it's super important. Your verse this week is another favorite of many: **Proverbs 3:5-6**.

❏ You are up to memory keys seven and eight! Can you recite the first six? More important, are you using them in your efforts to hide God's Word in your heart? The next two keys are as important as the rest, so read this week's **Practical Suggestions** carefully. Try writing out from memory all the keys we have studied so far at least once this week—in order. Can you do it?

My tongue shall speak of thy word:
For all thy commandments are righteousness.
Psalms 119:172

The Road Ahead
Survival Kit > Week 4 > Bible Search

Welcome back to another study in Christian survival. This Bible Search looks at how God leads and directs in the life of a Christian. Often the little decisions we make have lasting consequences—and much more so the big ones! How encouraging then, to know God is willing to lead us through them all.

> *Trust in the Lord with all thine heart; and lean not unto thine own understanding. In all thy ways acknowledge him, and he shall direct thy paths. Proverbs 3:5-6*

1. What is one privilege of being a child of God? Romans 8:14

> *Note: Life is filled with perplexity and distress. Yet, praise God, He is willing to guide us as His own sons and daughters.*

2. How would you summarize God's desire for each of us? Colossians 1:9

> *Note: To be filled with a knowledge of God's will is to be filled with a knowledge of His Word—for God's will is found in the Bible. This is one reason Scripture memory is so vitally important!*

3. What is the primary way God seeks to direct us?

   Psalms 119:33-35

   Psalms 119:59-60

   Psalms 119:97-100

   Psalms 119:116-117

   Psalms 119:133

   Note: God's counsel on any topic can be researched in the Scriptures. If you seek, you will find.

4. How does the Spirit often lead us?

   Isaiah 30:21

   John 14:26

   Note: God often flashes verses of Scripture we have memorized into our mind in specific situations at just the right time, to give us the exact guidance we need.

5. How thoroughly does God want to direct us in each of the following areas?

   Actions: I Corinthians 10:31

   Words: Ephesians 4:29

   Thoughts: Philippians 4:8

   Note: God is so committed to our success He is willing to give us direction in even the smallest details of life. With guidance like that, who can fail?

6. What is sometimes necessary in order to discern God's direction through the word?

   Lamentations 3:25

   Hosea 12:6

   Micah 7:7

   Note: If you are facing a tough decision, make it a point to spend some extra time seeking God through the Word and wait on Him to speak. If you must make a decision—do the best you can, based on the principles God has given you through His Word up to that point.

7. What should we do when our "impressions" seem to contradict the Word?

   Isaiah 8:20

   Proverbs 19:21

   Note: If you sense God directing you to do something that violates a principle of His Word, you can be pretty sure it's not God!

8. What will be the results of allowing God to direct in our life? Deuteronomy 28:1-2

What a wonderful thought—the wisdom of the Almighty is available to us! He who knows the thoughts and intents of every heart, and who sees tomorrow as clearly as today is willing to guide our steps through every perplexity and trial. What's more, His great love for us and interest in our success, give the assurance His leading is always for our best. What about you? Are you willing to seek the Lord's guidance for your life? To search the Scriptures and then pursue His revealed will? There is no better guidebook!

❏ Yes   ❏ No

The Road Ahead
Survival Kit > Week 4 > Practical Suggestions

Many people, when they first begin to grasp how powerful the memory keys you have been studying really are, become so excited about memorizing, that they make a big mistake. They start trying to memorize too much—maybe they set out to memorize a long list of verses on specific topics. Or they try to learn whole chapters, or even whole books of the Bible. While these are noble endeavors, what typically happens is things soon degenerate to rote memorization—and there's little or no impact on the life. We recommend instead focusing on key verses that are intimately intertwined with your own personal walk with God. Here is what we mean:

Key #7. Memorize Fresh Verses.

> *And these words, which I command thee this day, shall be in thine heart. Deuteronomy 6:6*

First, ask God to begin pointing out specific verses He wants you to memorize. If you are spending time with God each morning, in prayer and Bible study, He has probably already begun impressing certain key verses on your heart. Maybe you have started noticing verses that you hear in a sermon, or perhaps some friend has a knack for sharing especially encouraging Scriptures. Maybe you have run across some interesting verses in these Survival Kit lessons. However God sends you verses—we recommend memorizing them while they are fresh. If possible, that same day!

When God speaks to our heart, He's saying something He wants us to remember. And He wants us to review those lessons, over and over, to ensure they make a lasting impact on our life. So we won't forget what He has taught us. See Deuteronomy 4:9. Rather than planning out what verses to memorize, learn to listen, and let God lead.

Assigned verses are fine—especially when starting out, but they should be supplemented with verses given you directly by God. And eventually you will want to make key verses you find entirely on your own, a bigger and bigger percentage of the verses you learn. It is these fresh, personal verses that will prove most meaningful in your life. So be alert. And learn to look for them morning by morning as you meet with the Lord.

Key #8. Stick to Short Passages.

Whom shall he teach knowledge? and whom shall he make to understand doctrine? them that are weaned from the milk, and drawn from the breasts. For precept must be upon precept, precept upon precept; line upon line, line upon line; here a little, and there a little. Isaiah 28:9-10

Though it is tempting, avoid trying to memorize long passages, such as whole chapters or books of the Bible—especially at first. Start with just a verse or two, here and there. This is how the Holy Spirit teaches—precept upon precept, line upon line, "comparing spiritual things with spiritual" (I Corinthians 2:13). You do not need to memorize an entire passage to understand the context of a single verse—and it is almost never necessary to quote a whole chapter to answer some friend's question or objection. Focus instead on memorizing key verses and then building those verses into your life. Longer passages are not only more challenging to memorize, but harder to review, and more difficult to retain.

Actually, there may be times you might want to try what I call verse trimming. That is, rather than memorizing, a long difficult verse, focus on memorizing just that part of the verse God impresses you to learn. Verses like Esther 4:14, and Zechariah 4:6, are long and difficult to learn—but there are choice parts in those verses that are very easy to learn and quite powerful. All of Scripture is important, but there's nothing inspired about our modern chapter and verse breaks—so feel free to choose your own breaks as God leads you. You'll accumulate more verses, more quickly.

You can always go back later, of course, and memorize the rest of some verse you have trimmed, or even try a longer passage if you like. For a passage, choose one with several parts you already know and simply fill in the missing pieces, one or two verses at a time. And make sure you follow all the principles we have talked about so far as you do—for each individual verse. Give special attention to each reference.

But again, be careful. Avoid attempting longer passages until Bible memorization has become a way of life, and you have several hundred verses under your belt to prove it! Your patience will be well rewarded.

Fellowship of Faith

Week #5

Fellowship of Faith
Survival Kit > Week 5 > Memo

F
A
S
T

Memo:

Hi! Welcome one last time to our FAST Survival Kit. We pray this program has been a blessing to you—giving you useful tools for surviving as a Christian.

These principles are so important, it is a good idea to review them regularly. Every few months skim through the lessons again. Or better yet, find a friend, and introduce them to this course. There is much more to the Christian life, but we must never lose sight of the basics!

And hopefully, by now, you are beginning to see Scripture memory as one of those basics. Over and over God instructs his children to hide the Word in their hearts: Deuteronomy 6:6, I Corinthians 15:1-2, Job 22:22, Proverbs 7:1-3, Colossians 3:16, etc.

But God does more than just command us to memorize—He blesses His Word, and makes it a blessing in our life. The Bible becomes so sweet we could never imagine giving it up! Friend, press forward. Get a good taste for yourself.

**The Editor,
Hid in Christ**

Fellowship of Faith
Survival Kit > Week 5 > Objectives

Name: _____ Initialed by: _____

Date: _____

[ ] Welcome to our fifth and final Bible Search. This study talks about one of the most important keys to success in the Christian life. We call it the **Fellowship of Faith**. To put it simply, we need one another. If we are serious about pressing forward—we must be serious about pressing together!

[ ] Your fifth memory verse is a bit longer than the others, but it is a good one: **Hebrews 10:24-25**. Start working on it early in the week. Also, make sure you have your other four verses down perfectly. Review, review, review! Just think, you will soon know your first full "handful" of verses! Don't stop with five though—there are plenty more where those came from!

[ ] Your last two memory keys are just ahead. Read carefully the **Practical Suggestions**, and then review them along with the other eight keys you have learned so far—until you can recite all ten, in order. Also, take a few moments to think about your plans to continue your memorization of the Word going forward. Are you committed to sticking with it? We hope so!

I will never forget thy precepts:
For with them thou hast quickened me.
Psalms 119:93

Fellowship of Faith
Survival Kit > Week 5 > Bible Search

Welcome to the last Bible Search in our Survival Kit program. This study deals with one more critical key to survival: Bible-centered fellowship. God did not design any of us to strike out on the Christian path alone. Rather, His plan is for us to enjoy rich spiritual relationships. Make sure connecting with fellow believers always stays an important part of your life!

> *And let us consider one another to provoke unto love and to good works: not forsaking the assembling of ourselves together, as the manner of some is; but exhorting one another; and so much the more, as ye see the day approaching. Hebrews 10:24-25*

1. What is the true purpose of Christian fellowship? Hebrews 10:24-25

> *Note: God knows we need the encouragement and exhortation of other Christians to succeed in the Christian life. This need will only increase as we draw nearer and nearer to the second coming of Jesus Christ.*

2. Why is this kind of fellowship so important? Hebrews 3:13-14

> *Note: It is dangerous to try and survive as a Christian on our own. Do what it takes to find faith inspiring Christian fellowship and get the encouragement and exhortation you need!*

3.   What is the purpose of exhortation? Ephesians 4:15

Note: Exhortation is simply saying those things that will help another person become more like Jesus. To be most effective, it should always spring from a heart of love.

4.   What should be the bond that connects believers together in fellowship? Colossians 3:14

Where does this come from? Romans 5:5

5.   Read I Thessalonians 2:7-13. What are some of the ways Paul's love for these believers can be seen?

-
-
-
-
-

6. How is Paul's love evident in I Thessalonians 3:5-11?

-
-
-
-
-

7. Evaluate your life. How does your love for your brothers and sisters in Christ, compare with the apostle Paul?

Note: Genuine fellowship is a precious privilege! But it does not happen by accident—it takes work, commitment, and effort to find and build strong relationships. Yes, friendship takes time, but the rewards are worth it.

8. What did Paul say would be the end result of learning to love one another? I Thessalonians 3:12-13

Note: Incredible! Paul longed to see the hearts of these new believers established in holiness—and he was convinced it would be love for one another that would accomplish it!

9. Read Matthew 22:36-39. What light do these verses shed on the importance of Christian fellowship?

Note: Christian fellowship stands at the intersection of the Bible's two greatest commandments: love for one another rooted in mutual love for God. What could be more important?

10. What are your plans to ensure you receive the blessings of ongoing Christian fellowship through the days ahead?

You have now completed the final Bible Search in our FAST Survival Kit. You have examined the joy-giving truth that God has a rich plan for your life, the transforming power of a Christ-centered mind, the secret to getting back up when you stumble into sin, how to discern God's direction when perplexed, and the blessings of genuine Christian fellowship. All are crucial if you want to survive—and thrive—in your Christian walk. Are you willing to commit yourself right now to building these five basic principles into your life?

❏ Yes   ❏ No

Fellowship
Survival Kit > Week 5 > Practical Suggestions

Welcome to our last two memory keys. Have they been helpful so far? Have you been successful in learning your verses? Can you quote them each word-perfect? Do you know their references? Are you meditating on your verses, and applying them to your life? How is your daily review coming? This week we will look at two more keys to Scripture memory—keys that will help you continue memorizing faithfully through the weeks and months to come. Study them with a prayer!

Key #9. Set a Pace.

> *Then said Jesus to those Jews which believed on him, If ye continue in my word, then are ye my disciples indeed; And ye shall know the truth, and the truth shall make you free. John 8:31-32*

More important than how determined you are to memorize right now—is how consistent you will be down the road. Will you still be memorizing five years from now? In five months? or even in five weeks? Two verses a week will become a thousand in ten years, but only if you are consistent—for ten years!

How do you stay consistent? Just this: set a pace. Start with one or two verses a week. If that becomes too easy, try setting a goal of three or four verses a week. The key is to make it a rule to NEVER memorize less than your goal. You can always memorize more—but you must not allow a single week to slip by when you memorize less. We're not talking your *average* number of verses. We're talking about a minimum goal that you meet every time...

If you need help picking verses to learn, we've got a handy resource for you at FAST. We call it our Minute Memorizer, and it consists of 52 choice starter verses you can learn in one minute or less. That's one verse a week for a year! To grab it, go to: *WWW.FAST.ST/MINMEM*. Think of it as our free gift to you for making it to the end of these studies!

We also have many more study guide courses just like this one, with more recommended verses. These courses are another great way to help keep you moving forward in your memorization.

Key #10. Get Some Accountability.

> *But exhort one another daily, while it is called To day; lest any of you be hardened through the deceitfulness of sin. For we are made partakers of Christ, if we hold the beginning of our confidence stedfast unto the end. Hebrews 3:13-14*

One of the biggest keys to success in Scripture memory, is longterm accountability. Don't risk going it alone! Without accountability, it is just too easy to slack off—first one week, and then another. Soon your whole Scripture memory program has crashed!

To avoid this, try finding a friend or two willing to meet with you weekly, and check up on your new verses. Better yet, find someone interested in memorizing alongside you, and check up on their verses too. You may also want to become part of a free Memory Club, online at FAST.

FAST, as you probably know, is an online community, with thousands of members from around the world. And our Memory Club is a great way to expand your local circle of support. We're constantly sharing new resources with our community, and we would love you to plug in. To do so, just visit us at *WWW.FAST.ST/CLUB*.

At some point you may even want to consider pulling together a small group in your church, and lead them through the Survival Kit—and then perhaps some of our more advanced training courses. Teaching the principles you've learned to others is a great way to establish them more firmly in your mind. For information about how to lead a FAST team, please check out our free Leaders Manual at *WWW.FAST.ST/LM*.

God's plan for you is to write His Word in your heart and mind. And He longs to do it. It's our prayer these lessons have given you the tools and training you need to cooperate with Him!

Ready to take the next step? Look for our Basic Training course, the next step in our Discipleship Track. Discover practical nuts and bolts keys to the foundational skills of discipleship, and deepen your walk with God. Your life may never be the same again!

Additional Resources

From FAST

FAST Missions
Cutting-Edge Tools and Training

Ready to become a Revival Agent? FAST Missions can help! Our comprehensive training curriculum will give you the skills you need to take in God's Word effectively, live it out practically, and pass it on to others consistently.

Eager to start memorizing God's Word? Our powerful memory keys will transform your ability to hide Scripture in your heart.

Want to explore the secrets of "real life" discipleship? Our second level of training zooms in on critical keys to growth, like Bible study, prayer, time management, and more.

Want to become a worker in the cause of Christ? Our most advanced training is designed to give you the exact ministry skills you need to spark revival and see it spread.

For more information, please visit us at:

WWW.FASTMISSIONS.COM

Study Guides

Looking for life-changing study guides to use in your small group or Bible study class? These resources have been used by thousands around the world. You could be next!

Survival Kit
Want to learn how to memorize Scripture effectively? These study guides will teach you 10 keys to memorization, all drawn straight from the Bible. Our most popular course ever!

Basic Training
Discover nuts and bolts keys to the core skills of discipleship: Bible study, prayer, time management, and more. Plus, learn how to share these skills with others! It is the course that launched our ministry.

Revival Keys
Now as never before, God's people need revival. And these guides can show you how to spark revival in your family, church, and community. A great revival is coming. Are you ready?

For more information about these and other study guides, please visit us at *http://fast.st/store*. Or look for these titles on Amazon.

Online Classes

Want to try out some of the resources available at FAST? Here is just a small sampling of courses from among dozens of personal and small group study resources:

Crash Course
Discover Bible-based keys to effective memorization.
http://fast.st/cc

Fact or Fiction
Does the Bible really predict future events? You be the judge.
http://fast.st/prophecy

Monkey Business
Find out how evolution, in fact, flunks the science test.
http://fast.st/monkey

Dry Bones
Want more of God's Spirit? Learn how to pursue revival.
http://fast.st/bones

The Lost Art
Rediscover New Testament keys to making disciples.
http://fast.st/lostart

For more information about these and other classes, please visit us at *http://fast.st/classes*.

Digital Tools

FAST offers a number of powerful "apps for the soul" you can use to grow in your walk with God. And many of these are completely free to anyone with an account. Some of these include:

Review Engine
Our powerful review engine is designed to help ensure effective longterm Bible memorization. Give it a try, it works!

Bible Reading
An innovative Bible reading tool to help you read through the entire Bible, at your own pace, and in any order you want.

Prayer Journal
Use this tool to organize important requests, and we'll remind you to pray for them on the schedule you want.

Time Management
Learn how to be more productive, by keeping track of what you need to do and when. Just log in daily and get stuff done.

For more information about more than twenty tools like these, please visit us at *http://fast.st/tools*.

Books

If the content of this little book stirred your heart, look for these titles by the same author.

For Such A Time...
A challenging look at the importance of memorization for the last days, including topics such as the Three Angel's messages and the Latter Rain.

Moral Machinery
Discover how our spiritual, mental, and physical faculties work together using the sanctuary as a blueprint. Astonishing insights that could revolutionize your life!

The Movement
Discover God's plan to finish the work through a powerful endtime movement. Gain critical insights into what lies just ahead for the remnant!

For more information about these and other books, please visit us at *http://fast.st/store*. Or look for these titles on Amazon.

Made in the USA
Middletown, DE
11 September 2023

38357835R00035